The Life of Plants

Plant Products

Richard & Louise Spilsbury

Heinemann
LIBRARY

Chicago, Illinois

© 2008 Heinemann Library
a division of Pearson Inc.
Chicago, Illinois

Customer Service 888-454-2279
Visit our website at www.heinemannraintree.com

Design: Victoria Bevan and Planman Technologies
Illustrations: Jeff Edwards
Printed and bound in China by CTPS

12 11 10 09 08
10 9 8 7 6 5 4 3 2 1

**Library of Congress Cataloging-in-Publication
Data**
Spilsbury, Louise
Plant products / Louise and Richard Spilsbury
     p. cm. -- (Life of Plants)
Includes bibliographical references (p.).
Summary: Surveys the many uses of plants,
including nutrition, fuel, building, gardening, and
medicine.
ISBN 978-1-4329-1503-2 (hbk)
ISBN 978-1-4329-1510-0 (pbk)
1. Food crops--Juvenile literature. 2. Plant
products--Juvenile literature. 3. Plants, Useful--
Juvenile literature. [1. Food crops. 2. Plant products.
3. Plants, Useful.] I. Spilsbury, Richard, 1963- II.
Title. II Series.
    SB175 .S65 2002
    630--dc21
                    2001008303

Acknowledgments

The publishers would like to thank the following
for permission to reproduce photographs:
© Christine Osbourne p. **28**; © Corbis pp. **5**, **18**,
21, **24**, **26**, **32**, **33**, **34**, **36**, **37**, **39**; © Gareth
Boden p. **14**; © George Hartwell, Calflora—
University of California p. **35**; © Holt Studios
pp. **6**, **7**, **8**, **9**, **10**, **12**, **13**, **15**, **17**, **19**, **22**, **23**,
27, **31**, **38**; © Oxford Scientific Films p. **16**;
© Peter Spilsbury p. **29a**, **29b**; © Photodisc
p. **19b**; © Science Photo Library pp. **11**, **25**,
Philippe Plailly/Eurelios p. **20**.

Cover photograph of cinnamon and spices on
wooden spoon reproduced with permission of
PhotoLibrary.com.

The publishers would like to thank Andrew
Solway and Ann Fullick for their assistance in
the preparation of this book.

Disclaimer

Contents

Plants for Life! 4

Fruits 6

Vegetables 8

Nuts and Seeds 10

Cereals 12

Beans and Peas 14

Drinks 16

Adding Flavor 18

Medicines 20

Perfumes and Essential Oils 22

Plant Power: Fuel from Plants 24

Building 26

In the Home 28

Clothing and Accessories 30

Paper 32

Cleaning Up 34

Conservation 36

Plants for Leisure 38

Try It Yourself! 40

Looking at Plant Products 42

Glossary 44

Further Information 47

Index 48

Any words appearing in the text in bold, **like this**, are explained in the glossary.

A plant may be called different things in different countries, so every type of plant has a Latin name that can be recognized anywhere in the world. Latin names are made of two words: the first is the genus (general group) a plant belongs to and the second is its species (specific) name. Latin plant names are given in parentheses throughout this book.

Plants for Life!

Plants are the key to all life on Earth. Everything that each animal (including you!) does—breathing, moving, eating, and even sleeping—requires **energy**. We get energy from our food, and all of the food we eat either comes from plants or relies on plants for its own food.

Plant producers

Plants are unique among living things because they can make their own food. For that reason we call them producers. In the process called **photosynthesis**, plants use the energy from sunlight to turn **carbon dioxide** from the air and water from the soil into a type of sugar, the food that gives them energy to live and grow.

Animal consumers

Animals cannot make their own food. They are consumers, which means that they consume (eat) plants or animals that eat plants. For example, when we eat **fruits** and vegetables, we take in the nourishment locked up in these plant parts and use it to make the energy we need. When we eat beef or drink milk, we are getting the plant's energy secondhand—after the cow that ate grass plants has taken it in!

The only source of energy available to life on Earth is the sun. So, all food chains, like this one, start with plants because only plants can convert sunlight into sugars.

The air that we breathe

When plants make their own food by photosynthesis, people benefit in other ways. During photosynthesis, plants release **oxygen** into the air. Oxygen is an essential gas for humans—we need to breathe in oxygen to carry out **respiration**. Respiration is the way living things get energy from their food. During respiration we release a gas called carbon dioxide. If the levels of carbon dioxide in the air were much higher, it would be poisonous to us. By absorbing (taking in) carbon dioxide to make their food, plants help to keep our air healthy.

That is why the trees that line city streets and fill green parks are so important to the health of people living in towns and cities. Tree leaves trap carbon dioxide, and they are particularly good at removing the tiny bits of soot poured into the air from car exhaust. This type of air **pollution** is a problem for people who have breathing difficulties, such as **asthma**.

Trees and other plants not only make our streets look more attractive, they act like a city's lungs, cleaning the air so people can breathe more easily.

Fruits

In science, a **fruit** is defined as the part of a plant that contains its **seeds**. Some fruits, such as oranges or blackberries, contain many seeds. Others, like grapes, have one or two seeds inside each juicy fruit. In apples, seeds grow inside a core within the fruit. Strawberries are unusual because their seeds grow on the outside of the fleshy fruit.

Fruit plants

The fruits we eat grow on different kinds of plants. Apples, cherries, plums, and oranges grow on trees. Blueberries, blackberries, and raspberries grow on bushy plants. Grapes grow on climbing **stems** that wrap around supports to grow tall. Strawberries grow on small plants close to the ground. Banana plants have long leaves that grow from an underground stem.

How do we get seedless grapes?

If fruits hold seeds, why can we buy seedless grapes? Grapes are grown from **cuttings**. The fruit grower cuts a piece of stem from an adult plant and grows it into a new plant identical to the first. At some time in the past, an odd grape plant must have grown without seeds. These sold well, so farmers produced more seedless grapes by growing new plants from cuttings of this one.

The bases of the leaves on a banana plant grow so tightly together they look like a tree **trunk**.

Where do fruits grow?

Some fruits grow best in countries with a **temperate** climate. These are countries that have a cold season every year. The most successful temperate fruits are apples, pears, plums, cherries, blueberries, strawberries, and grapes. **Citrus fruits**, such as oranges, lemons, and grapefruit, need warm temperatures most of the year. Some fruits, such as bananas, pineapples, mangoes, papayas, and guavas, can only grow in the **tropics**.

Eating fruit

Many fruits taste sweet because they are designed to tempt animals to eat them and so help disperse (spread) the plant's seeds. The natural sugars in fruit are essential for animals like us. Our bodies can turn them into **energy** easily and quickly.

Fruit is also the best source of **vitamin** C you can eat. This important vitamin helps to keep your blood and teeth healthy, heals your wounds, and helps to protect you against colds. Fruit also contains **fiber**. As fiber passes through your body, it keeps your digestive system clean and healthy.

Oranges are one of the world's most popular fruits. Most of the oranges in this orchard in Florida will be **processed** into fruit juice.

Olive oil

The olive oil we use for cooking and to make salad dressings comes from olives, which are fruits of the olive plant. Around 9 to 11 pounds (4 to 5 kilograms) of olives are crushed to make just 34 ounces (1 liter) of olive oil.

Vegetables

Peas, carrots, potatoes, broccoli, eggplant, celery—the list of vegetables we eat is seemingly endless. We eat some vegetables fresh, while we buy others canned or frozen. We eat some raw, while we always cook others first. Vegetables are eaten in hundreds of different ways and are a very important part of people's diets all over the world.

What is a vegetable?

A vegetable is a plant that is eaten whole or in part, raw or cooked, usually with a main meal or in a salad, but not usually as a dessert. In some cases we eat the underground parts of the plant: carrots are a kind of **root**, potatoes are **tubers**, and onions are **bulbs**.

Fruit or vegetable?

Some of the plant parts you see in the vegetable section of your supermarket are actually **fruits**. We think of tomatoes, peppers, and eggplants as vegetables because we cook them in savory dishes like stews and casseroles, but in scientific terms they are fruits. A fruit is the part of the plant that grows around its **seeds**. This confusion happens the other way around, too: we think of rhubarb as a fruit because we cook it in desserts, but it is the leaf stalk of a plant, so it is really a vegetable!

Some of the vegetables we buy may be grown locally. Others may be **imported** from countries far away.

Some vegetables are the tasty leaves of different plants, such as watercress, spinach, and chard. Celery sticks are leaf **stalks**, and asparagus and bamboo shoots are parts of **stems**. We also eat flowers, such as broccoli, and **buds**, such as brussel sprouts.

Good for you!

Plants contain **energy**, which they make from **photosynthesis**, but they also take up **nutrients** from the soil (through their roots). When we eat plant parts, we take in these nutrients. Fresh vegetables contain nutrients such as **vitamin** C. They also give us **minerals** such as **calcium** and **iron**, which our bodies need to grow strong and healthy. Vegetables also contain **carbohydrates**, one of the body's main sources of energy.

Vegetables from the sea!

Most of us eat sea vegetables every day, though we don't know it! Manufacturers use them as thickeners in products such as ice cream, salad dressings, and even toothpaste. You can also eat sea vegetables in meals. Thin, dry sheets of nori seaweed (*Porphyra lanceolata*) are used in Japanese soups and to wrap sushi (little wraps of rice and raw fish).

These potatoes are being harvested. Potatoes are the potato plant's underground food store. They are full of carbohydrates, which means they give us lots of energy.

Nuts and Seeds

Nuts are **seeds** covered with a hard shell. Most are the seeds of trees. The part we eat, which we often call the nut, is actually the kernel—the seed inside the shell. Nuts and other seeds are the parts that can grow into new plants. Seeds contain food that the new plant can use to make the **energy** it needs for its first days of growth. This food store is rich in **protein** and **fat**, making it a useful source of **nutrients** for us, too.

You can buy nuts in their shell or with shells removed. Nuts can be eaten in many ways: whole, flaked, or ground, or turned into nut butters. Many nuts are roasted and eaten as snacks or added to savory meals and sweet foods such as puddings, cakes, and cookies.

Types of nuts

The biggest nut in the world is the coconut. You can eat the white flesh inside the brown husky shell, fresh or dried. Almond nuts are one of the most popular nuts. In fact, coconuts and almonds are really the "stones" of **fruits**. The coconut has a fibrous outer fruit, and the almond has a leathery one.

The peanut plant is related to peas and beans, but the **pods** grow underground. This is why they are sometimes called groundnuts.

Pecan nuts are true nuts. They are enclosed in a thick green husk that splits open when ripe. Chestnuts grow inside spiny seed cases. White, bean-shaped cashew nuts are unusual because they grow in shells that dangle from the end of fruit-like parts known as cashew apples.

Seed surprises

In addition to nuts, we eat many other types of seeds, from tiny white sesame seeds to flat green pumpkin seeds. Many seeds are crushed to remove their **oils**. Oils from flaxseeds and sunflower seeds are used for cooking oil and in margarine. Some, such as sunflower and pumpkin seeds, are roasted in oil and salt to make a snack food.

Some seeds, such as sesame seeds, have a great variety of uses in cooking. Whole sesame seeds decorate cakes and breads. Sesame oil is used in many Asian dishes. Sesame seed paste, called tahini, is used in a savory spread called hummus. Sesame seeds are also crushed with sugar to make a dessert called halva.

Under the microscope

Seed oils for a healthy heart?

Cholesterol is a type of fat. Heart disease seems to be linked to levels of this fat in the blood. High levels mean the blood vessels that feed the heart muscle can get blocked. This image shows a blockage in a human **artery** (see arrow). Doctors have discovered that oils made from some plant seeds can actually lower and balance the levels of cholesterol in the blood. This can help to protect people against heart disease. Olive oil is a good choice, and corn oil, sunflower oil, and flaxseed oil are even better. Plant oils are a healthy addition to everyone's diet.

Cereals

If people told you that they eat grass for breakfast, you would probably think they were a little crazy. Yet you probably do just the same thing yourself! Most of the breakfast cereals we eat each morning are made from the **seeds** of different kinds of grass plants.

Cereals are members of the grass **family** of plants. The seeds of cereal plants are called grains and are used to make many of the world's most useful foods. Some of the most important cereals include wheat, maize (corn), rice, rye, oats, barley, and millet. Some cereal grains, such as rice, are eaten in a form much like how they come off the plant. Some, such as wheat, are ground into flour, which in turn can be used to make bread, pasta, or puddings. Corn, rice, and wheat grains are **processed** to make breakfast cereals.

Wheat wonders

Wheat is the most important food for most of the world's population. Wheat plants cover more of Earth's surface than any other food crop. In one year the world's farmers grow enough to fill a train stretching around the world more than 20 times!

These unripe wheat plants will eventually turn golden brown and grow to about 5 feet (1.5 meters) tall.

Cereal plants

Cereal plants are efficient food producers because they grow and make seeds quickly. Lots of plants can be grown closely together so that one field of plants can produce a large amount of grain. The grains (seeds) we eat come from a cluster of flowers at the top of the cereal plant, called a spikelet. Grass plants are **wind pollinated**, so they do not need colorful flowers to attract insects for **pollination**. Instead, they have green leaf-like scales around the flower parts that will grow the seeds.

Good for you!

Inside a seed there is a tiny **embryo**, but most of the space is taken up with stored food. The food is there to make **energy** for the embryo to **germinate**. When we eat seeds, we get the benefit of this valuable food store. Grass seeds such as corn, wheat, rice, and rye are **nutritious** because they store **proteins** and **carbohydrates**, which give you energy and keep you healthy.

Rice

Rice is a staple (very important food) for more than half the people of the world. People in Asia have grown rice for food for over 5,000 years. Some rice is still grown on terraces (hilly patches surrounded by mud walls to keep water in) built around 2,000 years ago. Rice is a unique type of cereal crop because it is the only one that grows with its roots underwater. The seedlings (young plants) are planted in paddy fields that are flooded with water.

Beans and Peas

Beans and peas are types of **seeds**. They belong to a large **family** of plants called **legumes**. Legumes are plants that grow their seeds in cases called **pods**. Beans and peas contain **vitamins** and a lot of **protein**.

Some beans are picked before they are fully developed, and eaten fresh. You can cook and eat the pods of some, such as scarlet runner beans (*Phaseolus coccineus*), with the seeds. Other beans, such as broad beans (*Vicia faba*), are removed from the pods first. Some beans are left to develop fully on the plant before being picked. These are often called dry beans because they are hard and can be stored for a long time. Dried peas, beans, and lentils are eaten all over the world.

Poisonous beans!

Dried beans are an important food, but some beans are poisonous. Red kidney beans are one example. The raw beans contain a chemical that can make you sick. It takes only four or five beans to cause sickness and diarrhea. To avoid poisoning you must soak the beans for several hours, replace the water, and then boil furiously for at least 10 minutes to break down the poison. Then cook the beans normally, so that they are soft, tender, and tasty—and definitely not poisonous!

Ways of growing

Some legume plants grow as bushes, but many grow as climbing plants, like peas. Most bean plants climb by twisting their main **stems** around another plant's stem for support. Pea plants have softer stems. They climb using tendrils, which are long, thin leaflets that grow from the leaves. These twist around other stems or the leaves of tall grasses to hold the plant up to the light.

There are many different kinds of peas, including black-eyed peas, chick peas, and snap peas. Some have lots of seeds in a single pod, while others have very few. For example, chickpeas only have one or two peas per pod. When you eat snap peas, you eat the pods as well as the peas inside. The most common type of pea is the green or garden pea, the type we eat as a vegetable with a main meal.

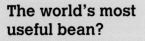

The world's most useful bean?

The soybean plant has small flowers and pods. The plant may not look very special, but its beans are incredibly versatile. You may know about tofu, soy sauce, and miso, but many other things we eat contain parts of soybeans, including many **processed** foods such as candies, baby foods, sausages, and burgers. Soybeans are also used to make **vegetarian** products that are chemically treated to look and taste like meat. Soybeans can even be used to make plastic bags that are **biodegradable,** rotting away in soil after they have been thrown away.

Drinks

People have made drinks from plants for thousands of years. You can take some drinks straight from the plant, such as the "milk" in a coconut. **Fruits** such as orange, apple, and pineapple are pressed to make fruit juices or blended with yogurt or ice cream to make smoothies or shakes. Different parts of plants are used to add flavor to fizzy drinks, such as lemon juice in lemonade.

Tea

Around half the people in the world drink tea. Most tea is made from the leaf tips of **evergreen** camellia bushes, which grow mainly on high, wet hills in Asia. The leaves are picked, dried, and crushed, and then soaked in boiling water to release their flavor. Different varieties of tea plants produce teas of different tastes. Sometimes fruits and other plant parts are added to create new flavors. The leaves of different plants, such as peppermint and chamomile, are used to make herbal teas.

The cow tree?

In parts of South America there is a tree that people can drink from. The cow- or milk-tree produces lots of sweet, white **sap** that oozes out from under its **bark** if it is cut. This creamy liquid tastes a bit like cow's milk!

Tea bushes grow in large areas called plantations. Pickers select the younger leaves because they give the best flavor.

Coffee

Coffee is made from coffee beans. Although they are called beans, they are really the **seeds** of berries that grow on a type of small tree found in hot, **humid** parts of the world. The berries are picked from the plant when they are ripe and then dried or soaked to remove their flesh. The two hard seeds inside are then roasted to release their flavor and smell. Coffee is made by grinding the roasted beans and mixing them with hot water. When this liquid has been strained, the coffee is ready to drink.

Drinking chocolate

The first people to enjoy chocolate drinks were the Mayans, who lived in Central America 1,400 years ago. They made a spicy drink by mixing water and chilli pepper with the roasted, crushed seeds of the cacao tree. Today, we use cacao seeds to make sweet chocolate drinks. The seeds are ground up to make a dark liquid. All seeds contain **fat**, and the fat (cocoa butter) in this liquid is removed to make cocoa powder. This can be mixed with sugar and milk to make drinking chocolate. If the cocoa liquid is mixed with sugar and extra cocoa butter, solid chocolate is the result!

Cacao fruits (**pods**) grow out of the **stem** of a tropical tree. They each contain 20 to 30 seeds. When the pods are ripe, the farmers split them open with long knives and scoop out the seeds.

Adding Flavor

We use lots of different plant parts to add flavor and color to our food, from the sugar we add to hot chocolate, the basil leaves we chop into sauces, and the pepper we grind into soup. People have been using herbs and spices to add flavor (and to disguise the taste of meat that was less than fresh) for thousands of years.

Spices

Spices come from a variety of different plant parts. Peppercorns are the sun-dried berries of the pepper vine. They are usually crushed or powdered before being added to food. Cloves are the dried **buds** of a tropical tree. Tangy-tasting ginger is the underground **stem** of another tropical plant. You can use ginger fresh (peeled), dried, or ground to add flavor to savory meals or cakes and puddings. Chillies are spicy fruits that are full of **seeds**. They are eaten fresh (in very small quantities) or dried to make chilli powder. The nutmeg tree provides us with two different spices. Nutmeg is the tree's seed. Mace is the fleshy network that surrounds the seeds. Both are ground and used in sweet and savory foods.

Herbs

Most herbs are the leaves or stems of certain plants that have distinctive flavors. Herbs can either be eaten fresh or dried, crushed into a powder, and stored in airtight containers so that they last longer.

Cinnamon is made from the **bark** of a tree that grows in India and Sri Lanka. The cinnamon sticks we buy are pieces of thin bark, cut from a young tree, that have curled up as they dried.

People use herbs to add flavor to savory dishes. For example, basil or oregano leaves taste good in tomato sauces. Chive **stalks** are used in salads or egg dishes. Mint leaves are used in sauces. Some herbs, such as parsley, are a good source of **vitamins** A and C, but you need to eat a lot of it to get the benefits of these.

Many herbs, such as mint, sage, oregano, and thyme, grow as small, bright green leaves on low-growing bushes. Dill plants are taller than many herb plants and their leaves are long and feathery. Most herbs are **perennial** plants, which live and flower for several years.

Sweet facts

We add sugar to our food and drinks to sweeten it and to bring out the flavor. Most of this sugar comes from sugar cane (top) or sugar beet (bottom). Sugar cane is a type of tall grass that grows in the **tropics**, and sugar is made from its stems. The sugar beet plant grows in **temperate** areas of the world, and sugar is made from its thickened **roots**. The sugar crystals extracted (taken out) from these very different plants look and taste just the same!

Medicines

Thousands of years ago, people discovered that plants could be used to treat illness. They figured out which plants could help with different health problems by trial and error, trying each one out until they found one that worked. Gradually people passed on their discoveries by word of mouth, and later they wrote them down. Many plants were even named according to the medicinal properties they have. Lungwort is used to help with some breathing problems and was named after the part of the body used for breathing—the lungs.

Today, many of the medicines we use are made from artificial (laboratory-made) chemicals, but most of the world's population uses plant medicines. Some may be used for fairly minor problems. For example, people breathe in **oil** from eucalyptus leaves to clear blocked noses when they have a cold. Other plants may be used to treat more serious conditions. Foxgloves are tall spikes of purple flowers. Their leaves contain a poison called digitalis, which deters small animals from eating them. Scientists use this poison to make a drug that helps the human heart beat more slowly and strongly. Some people with heart problems owe their lives to this common plant.

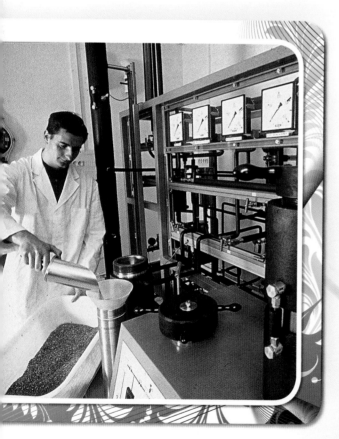

Some chemicals produced by plants, like the anti-cancer drug Taxol, made from the Pacific yew (*Taxus brevifolia*), can successfully treat some illnesses.

Other medicinal plants

Another very poisonous plant that can be used to our advantage is belladonna, also known as deadly nightshade. A drug called atropine is made from the berries of the belladonna plant. It is used to dilate (widen) the pupils of the eyes when they are being checked or operated on, and also to treat stomach problems.

Other medicines come from the **stems**, **roots**, or **bark** of plants. The **sap** from the stem of an opium poppy is used to make tablets such as codeine, which reduce the discomfort of headaches or other pains.

The root of ginseng, a plant related to ivy, has been used in China for thousands of years. The root is ground to a powder, and many people say that it has helped them recover from illness and relieved headaches and tiredness, among other problems. It is the bark of the cinchona tree of South America that is used to make quinine, a treatment for malaria, one of the most terrible diseases in the world today.

Records suggest that the Chinese identified more than 350 plants that could be used to make medicines as much as 5,000 years ago! Recent studies have found that today 75 to 80 percent of the world's population still uses plant medicines.

Perfumes and Essential Oils

Many of the scents we use in perfumes, bath oils, shampoos, and creams come from plants. Plant scents are stored in the form of **oils**, known as essential oils. Plants contain oils for a number of reasons. Some plants use sweet scents to attract insects or other animals to help them **pollinate** their flowers. Some plants use strong-smelling scents for the opposite reason—to repel (force away) animals that might want to eat them. In some cases, the oils protect the plant from disease, stopping them from becoming infected by germs that may invade through a damaged **stem**.

Aromatherapy

Aromatherapy is the use of plant oils to treat people's problems and make them feel better. Oils may be heated so their scent fills the air, added to bath water, or used on the skin. The different oils help people in different ways. For example, lavender is a calming scent and the oil helps to heal burns. Orange relaxes and refreshes you. Rosemary can help with breathing problems.

Lavender produces scented oil in both its leaves and its flowers.

Plants make their scents in different parts. A rose has scented oil in its **petals**, the eucalyptus tree has it in its leaves, cinnamon has it in its **bark**, garlic has it in its **bulbs**, and sandalwood trees have it in the heart of their **trunks**. Oranges make three slightly different scented oils in their flowers, leaves, and rind.

Extracting oils

Most oils are extracted (taken out) using steam. When steam is forced through plant parts, the heat makes the droplets of oil and water inside the plant **evaporate** (turn into a gas called **vapor**). The vapor is collected and cooled so it turns back into liquid oil and water. Oils from **citrus fruits**, such as orange, are extracted by "cold pressing." The rind is removed, ground up, and pressed to squeeze out the oils. Some perfumes are expensive because it takes a lot of plant material to make a little oil. To make 34 ounces (1 liter) of rose oil, it takes the flowers of 100,000 roses!

Tea tree tales

You do not make tea from the tea trees (*Leptospermum*) of Australia! Oil extracted from the leaves of the tea tree is one of nature's finest **antiseptics**. It was used by native Aborigine tribes in Australia to fight **infections** for thousands of years. Explorer Captain Cook gave the tea tree its English name in 1768. He stewed its leaves in hot water (like tea) for his crew to drink to prevent a disease called scurvy.

Plant Power: Fuel from Plants

We rely on fuel for almost everything we do. We use fuel to cook our food, heat and light our homes, and power our cars and computers. At one time, wood was the world's main source of fuel. In many countries wood is still the most important fuel: around nine out of ten people in developing countries rely on burning wood for heating and cooking. Wood is the most obvious fuel to come from plants, but did you know that coal, oil, and natural gas also come from plants?

Fossil fuels

Coal, oil, and gas are often called fossil fuels. Fossils are the remains of dead plants and animals that lived around 300 million years ago. As they rotted away and broke down, the **energy** inside some of them became stored in another form. Take the story of coal. Ancient plants trapped the sun's energy to make their food by **photosynthesis**, just as plants do today. When they died and their remains broke up in the soil, some of that energy was buried with them. In swampy areas plants decay very slowly, and dead, rotting plants piled up and crushed together to form **peat**, which can be burned.

The coal being dug from this mine in Russia formed from plants that died millions of years ago.

Gradually, layers of clay, sand, and stones got washed on top of the peat. Over millions of years the weight of these layers crushed the peat so much that it became hard and turned into coal. Oil and gas were created in much the same way, but in areas that were not swampy. Heat, **bacteria**, and the weight of layers of rock above turned the remains into oil or gas, trapped below ground.

When we burn oil, gas, and coal we release the stored energy as heat. The heat can be used to make steam to turn **turbines** to make electricity. Useful though they are, there is only a limited amount of fossil fuels, and they will eventually run out.

New plant fuels

Fossil fuels take millions of years to form, so once they are gone they cannot be used again. The oil from which we get gasoline will run out one day, so scientists are looking for alternatives to power our cars. Plants such as sugar cane and corn are loaded with sugars. Plant sugars can be collected and turned into an alcohol, called **ethanol**, that can be used as a fuel. A number of buses in Sweden and cars in Brazil already run on sugarcane alcohol. There has also been research into using plant **oils** from vegetables or beans, such as the soybean, as fuels. This technician is working at a factory where sugar juices are transformed into ethanol.

Building

Around the world many different plants are used for building. Some cottages still have thatched roofs made from straw, the dried **stalks** of a grass plant. In parts of the Middle East people build homes and boats from reeds. In Indonesia some roofs are made from banana leaves. The bamboo plant is used for many houses and bridges in parts of Asia. However, the plant people use most for building is the tree.

Wood

In order to support their height and the weight of their leaf-laden branches, trees have incredibly strong **stems** called **trunks**. As a tree grows taller, its trunk grows wider. The area of growth is just under the **bark**. The old wood inside the trunk is dead, and as it dries up it becomes hard and tough.

Wood is used in many building projects, in frames for windows and supporting walls for houses, and to make sheds, tools, furniture, and boats. It is useful because it is hard and strong. Also, it can be cut or carved into many (often intricate) shapes; it is strong but also springy; it does not rust, as many metals do; and if it is correctly looked after, wood can last for hundreds of years.

Bamboo is a type of grass that has tough woody stalks, making it an ideal building material. Bamboo scaffolding is used for almost all building and repair jobs in Hong Kong.

From tree to timber

"**Timber**" is the word used to describe "useful wood." People usually divide timber into **softwoods** and **hardwoods**. Softwoods come from **coniferous** trees such as spruce or pine. Hardwoods are more expensive because they come from slower-growing **broad-leaved** trees, such as oak.

In the forest, power saws are used to fell (cut down) trees and slice off their branches. Because trees are alive when they are cut down, the trunks still contain a lot of **sap** and are quite wet inside. If the trunks were cut into planks when wet, the pieces would shrink and warp (bend) as they dried out. Logs are usually dried out (seasoned) first, either in air or in warm rooms, to speed up the process. Then the bark is ripped off and the seasoned timber is sliced into planks or boards, ready to be used for building work.

Cheap woods

Big planks of wood can be expensive, so manufacturers make cheaper substitutes. Plywood and blockboard are made by sticking lots of thin sheets of wood together. Chipboard and fiberboard are made out of tiny chippings of wood or sawdust mixed with glue, all crushed together to form large boards. Veneers are thin sheets of expensive wood that cover chipboard so it looks like solid wood.

This house is made from timber. The wooden frame is covered in overlapping planks.

In the Home

If you look around your home, you may be able to see lots of things made from plants, from wooden tables to woven baskets. Different plant materials are suitable for different objects. The wood used to make a table is chosen for its strength and also for the way it looks. Willow or bamboo **stems** are used to make baskets because they are soft enough to weave together, but they harden as they dry.

Wood colors and grains

The **timber** you get from each tree is different, both in color and pattern (grain). When a **trunk** is cut down its length to make planks for furniture, the tree's **annual rings** show up as attractive, curling lines called grains. Walnut wood has a particularly attractive grain; cherry wood is reddish like its fruit; mahogany is a very rich, dark brown wood; and oak is very tough but has an attractive grain.

Hardwoods

Some **hardwoods** used for furniture, such as mahogany and teak, grow in **rain forests**. So many have been cut down in the past that they are now very rare. Hardwoods grow very slowly, so it is not easy to replace them. Today, laws protect many of the hardwood forests that remain. These hardwood trees are growing in a rain forest in Indonesia.

Under foot

There are many plant materials that can be used for flooring, including **fibers** such as seagrass, coir, jute, and sisal. In the **tropics**, people use strips of coconut palm leaves to make mats. The coconut husk is made up of short, stiff fibers (called coir) that can be woven together to make mats, ropes, and brooms.

Sisal (*Agave sisalana*) is another plant grown for its strong fiber. Sisal fiber is obtained from the plant's sword-like leaves, which can grow to 2 to 6 feet (0.6 to 1.8 meters) long. The leaves are crushed to squeeze out any soft plant material and juices, and then the coarse fibers are scraped, washed, and dried. Sisal is used to make rope, doormats, and rugs. Today, sisal is mostly grown in dry regions of Brazil, Tanzania, Angola, Kenya, and Madagascar.

This man is preparing a crop of coconuts.

Houseplant tips

Most of us also like having live plants in the home. Before choosing a new houseplant, look at the room you will be putting it in. Is it dry or **humid**, and how light is it? In the store, check the plant's label to see what it needs—for example, light and temperature are most important for flowering plants. Does the plant need sunlight through a window or a constant temperature? Some house plants are very particular about soil and **fertilizer** (plant food), so you may need to buy these, too.

Coir mats are made from the hairy brown husk of the coconut.

Clothing and Accessories

Take a look at the labels inside your clothes. Chances are that at least one of the things you are wearing started life as a plant! Many clothes and accessories across the world are made from plants.

Fibers and fabrics

Some fabrics are made of **fibers** from plant parts. Plant fibers are useful because they are strong but flexible enough to weave together. Flax fibers come from the **stem** of the flax plant (*Linum Usitatissimum*). They are extracted by soaking and beating the plant and are then woven together to make linen. Panama hats are made of young leaf fibers from the **shoots** of the straw palm (*Carludovica palmata*). Leaves from the raffia palm (*Raphia farinifera*) make raffia, a fiber woven to make baskets and hats.

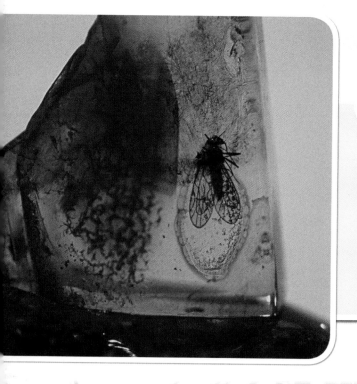

Amber jewelry

Amber is actually **resin** that seeped from fir and pine trees around 50 million years ago. As it hardened, it formed the bronze gemstone used for jewelry today. Some pieces of amber even have insects inside, trapped in time as the oozing resin flowed over them.

Cotton

Many people across the world wear cotton clothes. Cotton fabric is light but strong, so cotton clothes, such as jeans, last a long time.

Cotton fibers come from the **pod** of the cotton plant (*Gossypium hirsutum*). The fluffy white fibers grow on the **seeds** inside the pods, and there are about 30 seeds inside each pod. When the seeds are ripe, the pods open up to reveal the fibers. Cotton pickers harvest the open pods (called bolls) before the fibers are blown away.

Even the longest cotton fibers are no more than 1.5 inches (4 centimeters) long. To make long reels of thread, a machine twists and spins many fibers together to make one long thread or yarn. Finally, two or more threads are woven together to make sheets of fabric.

Tree silk?

Rayon fabric is sometimes called "tree silk" because it is made from **cellulose**, a chemical in wood. To make rayon, wood is chemically treated to dissolve the cellulose so that it forms a liquid. It is then forced through tiny holes in a machine to make sticky threads. When these harden they can be woven together to make fabric.

The cotton plant grows cotton fibers so that its seeds will be more easily caught by the wind and blown onto new soil where some of them might grow.

Paper

How many products made of paper or cardboard can you think of? You are reading a book made from paper right now. You could list writing paper, newspapers, magazines and comics, wrapping paper, packing products, greetings cards, currency (money), bathroom and kitchen papers, and wallpapers. Paper is an essential part of our everyday lives, and it comes from plants.

From plant to page

Most modern papers are mainly made of **cellulose** taken from wood, usually from **softwood** trees such as pines and firs. Around half of the wood pulp used to make paper comes from wood chips. Wood chips are waste woods left over from cutting **timber** for other uses, such as building.

To make paper, **bark** is stripped off the logs and the wood is broken into tiny pieces (cellulose **fibers**) in a big machine. Then the fibers are mixed with chemicals and water to make wood pulp. The wet pulp is poured onto a conveyor (moving) belt that is made of wire mesh. As the belt moves along, water drains through the mesh, leaving the damp paper fibers on the surface.

Past papers

People have used some form of paper for thousands of years. In fact, the word "paper" comes from the Egyptian word "papyrus," a type of reed plant from which ancient Egyptians made a type of writing material. The Chinese invented the first real paper sometime before 100 CE.

On a conveyor belt, wet wood pulp already looks a little like the paper it will become.

The conveyor then passes the wet paper fibers through rollers. These squeeze out more water and crush the fibers so that they stick together. To completely dry out the paper, the conveyor runs it through hot rollers, and as it comes out dry it is wound onto a giant reel in one endless sheet.

Different types of paper

Other fibers such as cotton, linen, hemp, and straw are also used to make paper, but these are less common. Different things can also be added to the wood pulp stage to create different types of paper. Chemicals give the paper a particular color or type of coating (such as a shiny finish). China clay can make the paper stronger. A chemical called "size" (which is actually **resin**) may be used to coat the paper, so that it does not become too absorbent. Dyes may be added to color it.

Waste not, want not— recycling paper

Millions of trees are cut down to make paper, and yet it is easy to recycle paper. When waste paper is soaked in water, it breaks back down into its original fibers. The ink can be washed off and the pulp used to make new paper products. Recycled paper is mostly used to make cardboard, napkins, newspapers, and even cereal boxes, but it can be used to make better quality paper, too.

Many different plant fibers can be used to make paper. This man, who lives in China, is using mulberry pulp.

Cleaning Up

Believe it or not, water by itself is not very useful for cleaning. Water has a property called surface tension, which means it runs off surfaces such as your skin. To see how surface tension works, place a drop of water on to a plastic or glass tabletop and watch how if forms a bead shape and does not spread out. This means it takes longer to wet a surface you want to clean. To make water useful for cleaning, we need to add a soap of some kind. When soap is added to water, surface tension reduces, so water spreads out and wets surfaces properly. Soap also attaches itself to any pieces of dirt, so that when you rinse off the soap, the dirt also gets washed away.

One of the main ingredients of soap is **fat**. Many soaps today are made using vegetable **oils** (a type of fat) such as olive oil, palm oil, sesame oil, and soybean oil. When the oils are heated with a chemical and salt, a soapy mixture floats to the surface. This is removed and pressed together to form soap.

Cleaning up contaminated ground

Plants can also help us clean up soils **contaminated** with toxic (poisonous) metals. Many plants cannot grow on contaminated soils but some, such as Indian mustard, poplars, sunflowers, and ferns, can.

One of the most unusual uses for members of the large lily plant **family** is soap.

When planted in contaminated areas, these plants suck up water containing dissolved toxic metals from the soil through their **roots**. The metals are carried to other plant parts, such as **stems**, **shoots**, and leaves. These parts can be cut and removed, leaving the ground clean.

Plants and sewage

Sewage is the waste water from household pipes—the stuff that washes down the drains from our kitchens and bathrooms. Many sewage systems use **algae** (small plant forms). Algae grow well in sewage because it is a good source of **nutrients** for them. The algae make **oxygen** (during the process of **photosynthesis**), which **bacteria** use to help them break down the waste in the water.

In reed bed sewage systems, plants are used in another cleansing stage. Marshy wetlands are used or created where reeds, cattails, and bulrushes thrive. As waste water flows through them, these plants act like a natural sieve (filter). Reed beds take longer to set up, but are much cheaper to run than ordinary sewage systems. Money is also saved because no pipes and tanks are required.

Mining with plants

In California, farmers are using *Streptanthus polygaloides* plants to mine **nickel**. If you grow these plants on nickel-rich soils, they absorb the metal. Farmers then burn the plants, producing ash. This ash is **smelted** and produces nickel. **Energy** produced during burning can also generate electricity. With the right soil, farmers can earn more money farming nickel than growing wheat!

Conservation

"Conservation" means the planned management of the natural world, the **habitats** of Earth, and the plants and animals that live in them. Although plants often require protection themselves, they also play an important role in conservation because they provide food and shelter for a whole variety of other plants and animals.

Countless insects, many too small for us even to see, eat the leaves of plants. Insects and other tiny creatures live on or in tree **bark**. Butterflies and other insects lay their eggs on plant leaves and **stems**. Birds, wild bees, monkeys, and squirrels live in holes or build nests in tall trees, to be safe from other animals. Trees also provide homes for other plants. In moist climates, mosses and ferns grow in trees. In the **tropics**, **bromeliads** and orchids live on high tree branches.

Panda protection

The giant panda is a good example of an animal that is vitally linked to its habitat. The panda is now an **endangered species**. That means that there are not many pandas left in the world, and one day the last may die out. One of the reasons for this is that pandas only eat bamboo, a tall grass, and humans are cutting down the bamboo forests where they live. An adult giant panda eats around 44 pounds (20 kilograms) of bamboo each day.

Erosion control

Erosion is the loss of soil as it is loosened and moved by wind, frost, rain, or water. The top layer of soil is particularly important to land, because it is rich in the **nutrients** that plants need to grow. Erosion is an important conservation issue in many countries of the world, and plants can help to solve the problem in different ways.

Plants can be used to protect areas of land or other plants by acting as windbreaks. Strong winds can cause real difficulties for farmers—storms can blow down crops or carry away soil from a field. A row of trees can provide a shield against even the strongest winds.

Roots not only hold plants firmly in the soil, they also hold the soil around the roots. Trees on a hillside can reduce the risk of landslides. Trees, such as willow (*Salix*) and alder (*Alnus*), which grow along riverbanks, develop a tangle of strong roots that hold the soil and reduce the amount of earth washed away from the bank by the moving water. Along sandy shores, the deep roots of marram grasses (*Ammophila arenaria*) prevent sands from shifting, and, as the grasses die and rot, they create a layer of humus (rich plant matter) in which other plants can grow.

Along the coast of the Netherlands, special grasses protect the sand dunes from erosion and the low lands beyond from the stormy North Sea.

Plants for Leisure

Plants not only provide us with many of life's necessities, they also give us many of the products we use for fun. Plants are involved in many of our leisure activities, from the grass fields we play games on to the canoes and boats we row or sail.

A baseball bat's handle is made from hickory (*Carya*) and ash (*Fraxinus*), two **hardwoods** that have long, solid **fibers** inside. This makes the bat strong. Wooden hockey sticks are traditionally made from mulberry (*Moraceae*), which is flexible but also strong.

Music and art

Some musical instruments, such as guitars and violins, have bodies made from wood. The black keys on some pianos are made from ebony (*Pithecellobium flexicaule*), a very hard and rare black wood that grows in African **rain forests**. Reeds used in the mouthpieces of saxophones and clarinets are cut from bamboo plants.

The pencil or charcoal you use for sketching comes from wood from trees. Wood surrounds the lead in your pencils, and charcoal is what is left behind after wood has been burned in a kiln. It can be squeezed together to make charcoal crayons.

The rubber used to make tires is the **sap** of rubber trees (*Hevea brasiliensis*). It is collected when the **bark** of the tree is cut.

Plants for pleasure

Without plants we would not exist. Plants provide us with the air we breathe and the food we eat. They clothe and shelter us. They are used to make drinks that quench our thirst, medicines that heal us, and scents that soothe us. Plants are the source of paper used to make the books, newspapers, and magazines that inform us. These things are all very important to our lives on this planet, but there is one other product of plant life that we have not yet mentioned—the pleasure plants give us.

People get a lot of satisfaction and pleasure from looking at plants, breathing in their scents, walking through woods, and growing their own plants, either for food or to bring color to their homes and gardens. For many of us, plants also mark the passing seasons. We know summer is making way for the fall when the leaves change color and begin to fall down. We know spring warmth will soon replace the chill of winter when the first flowers burst into bloom. Plants not only help to keep us alive, they also make our lives more pleasurable.

At a time when many of us live in busy cities, parks and gardens provide us with a place to rest or play, while enjoying the colors and scents of the plants within them.

Try It Yourself!

Try some of the activities on this page to make some of your own products from plants and also your own food chain.

Create a food chain

Food chains show us how the **organisms** (living things) in a **habitat** depend on one another for food. One food chain, for example, might show a plant that is eaten by a mouse, which in turn is eaten by an owl. Look back at the food chain on page 4 of this book for an example. You can make your own food chains using pictures that you draw or cut from magazines.

You will need:

• Old magazines with plant and animal pictures

• Scissors

• A pen or pencil

• Glue

• Paper

Choose a top predator, such as a lion, fox, or eagle. Find out what animal it eats. Then find out what that animal eats. Keep going until you get down to a plant. You have found a food chain! Cut out pictures of the animals and plants you have researched to make your own food chain. Stick them onto a sheet of paper and draw lines between them to show how it works. If you cannot find the pictures you want, try drawing your own.

Make your own lemonade!

Using fresh ingredients to make your own food or drinks is a good way to get the most **vitamins** and **nutrients** from your food. This is a simple recipe for a tangy, tasty drink.

You will need:

• 2 tablespoons lemon juice

• 1½ tablespoons lime juice

• 2 tablespoons granulated sugar

• 6 ice cubes

• 2 cups cold water

Squeeze the juice you need from fresh lemons and limes. Pour the juice into a jug. Then add the sugar and stir until dissolved. (The sugar becomes part of the juice.) Add the ice cubes and water and stir. Pour it into two glasses and serve.

Make a scented pomander

Scented room sprays were not available in the past, so people made their own room fresheners, called pomanders, using natural scents. These were made out of oranges and cloves and were hung in cupboards. Today, they are still given as gifts.

You will need:

- 1 orange
- 20 cloves
- A fork or toothpick
- Muslin, or other lightweight mesh fabric
- Ribbon

Use the fork or toothpick to make holes in the orange. You can make the holes in straight lines or in a pattern. Put a clove into each of the little holes. Then wrap the orange in a square of the muslin. Attach the ribbon to the top of the muslin and make a loop, so that the ribbon can be slipped over a rail or coat hanger.

As the orange dries, the fragrance from the **oils** in its rind is released, mixed with the spicy scent of the cloves.

Carrot and apple soup

It is important to eat many **fruits** and vegetables to stay healthy. This soup recipe contains both fruits and vegetables, making it delicious and good for you. Ask an adult to help you.

You will need:

- 1 pound carrots
- 1 onion
- 1 potato
- 1 large cooking apple
- 3½ tablespoons butter
- 4¼ cups vegetable stock
- Salt and pepper to taste

Peel and chop the vegetables into small pieces and cook them in the butter in a large pan for about 5 minutes. Peel and chop the apple and add to the pan. Add the rest of the ingredients. When the soup is boiling (bubbling furiously), put on the lid, turn down the heat a little, and let it cook for about 30 minutes. After that, let it cool down before you blend it in a blender (bit by bit) to make a smooth soup. When you are ready to eat, warm the soup up again in the pan.

Looking at Plant Products

Types of hardwoods and softwoods

Deciduous hardwoods

Deciduous hardwoods are the trees that lose their leaves in winter. They generally grow in regions with **temperate** climates, including Europe, Japan, New Zealand, Chile, and the central United States. Examples of deciduous hardwoods are oak, ash, elm, beech, birch, sycamore, and chestnut.

Evergreen hardwoods

Evergreen hardwoods are trees that keep their leaves all the year round. They generally grow more quickly than deciduous trees and to a larger size. They are usually softer and easier to work than deciduous trees. Most evergreens are found in tropical or sub-tropical regions such as South America, Central America, Africa, Myanmar (Burma), India, and the East and West Indies. Examples of evergreen hardwoods are mahogany, teak, African walnut, afrormosia, ebony, and balsa.

Softwoods

Softwoods are produced by the cone-bearing (**coniferous**) trees. They are generally evergreen and have needle-like leaves. They grow in regions with cold or cool temperate climates such as Canada, Scandinavia, and northern Russia. They grow much more quickly than hardwoods and are cheaper, softer, and easier to work. Their **seeds** are held in cones. Common examples are pine, fir, spruce, larch, cedar, and redwood.

Top crops!

Do you have any idea which **fruits** and vegetables are the most popular in the world? These lists tell you which of these crops are produced most across the world.

Top world fruit crops (2005):

1 Tomatoes
2 Watermelons
3 Bananas
4 Grapes
5 Apples

Top world vegetable crops (2005):

1 Sugar cane
2 Potatoes
3 Sugar beet
4 Soybeans
5 Sweet potatoes

Cereal crops

Cereals are types of grasses. Important cereals include wheat, rice, corn, barley, sorghum, oats, millet, and rye.

Wheat is one of the world's most important food crops. In many areas of the world, wheat appears in some form at nearly every meal. Most of these foods are made from the kernels (seeds or grains) of the wheat plant. The kernels are ground into flour to make breads, cakes, cookies, crackers, macaroni, spaghetti, breakfast cereals, and other foods. The leading wheat-producing countries include Canada, China, France, India, Russia, and the United States.

Corn (also called maize) kernels can simply be cooked and eaten, but they are also used to make breakfast cereals, baked products, salad dressings, and many other foods. When people eat eggs, meat, and dairy products, they benefit from corn indirectly, because large amounts of corn are fed to livestock.

Rye is a cereal grain similar to wheat and barley. The plant has slender seed spikes with long, stiff awns (beards). Rye is used to make bread and certain types of liquor. The heavy, black bread of Europe is made from rye. Rye is an important crop in the cool climates of northern Europe, Asia, and North America. Russia is the world's leading rye-growing country.

Rice is eaten by over half of the people in the world as the main part of their meals. Rice is usually grown in flooded fields. The water also kills weeds and other pests. Rice grows best in shallow water and thrives in many tropical areas because of the warm, wet climate. China and India grow more than half of the world's rice.

Oats are an important grain crop. Farmers grow them to feed livestock, but the seeds of oat plants are **processed** and used in foods such as oatmeal, oatcakes, and breakfast cereals. Oats are rich in starch and high-quality **protein**, and they provide a good source of **vitamin** B1. Russia is the leading oat-growing country.

Millet is an important source of food in Africa and Asia. People grind the seeds into flour for flat breads and thin, fried cakes. They also use the seeds in porridge. Millet seeds, leaves, and **stems** can be used as livestock feed.

Sorghum is grown for its round, starchy seeds. In India, Africa, and China, the grain is ground and made into pancakes or mush for food. In some countries it is used for feeding animals.

Barley is made into malt and is used in alcoholic drinks (such as beer), malted milk, and flavorings. Barley flour may be used in baby cereal and in bread. Barley is also used for animal feed. Russia is the leading producer of barley.

Glossary

algae type of plant that does not have leaves, stems, roots, or flowers. We call them a type of plant because they can use sunlight to make their own food during photosynthesis.

annual ring ring you can see when the trunk of a tree is cut down. If you count annual rings, you can find out a tree's age.

antiseptic substance that destroys or stops the growth of germs

artery thick-walled tube that carries blood away from the heart to other parts of the body

asthma lung disease causing periods of breathlessness, wheezing, and coughing

bacteria tiny organisms in the soil, water, and air. Some types of bacteria can bring about decay in dead plants and animals.

bark tough outer skin of a tree

biodegradable having the capacity to rot away in soil or sun after being thrown away. Things that are not biodegradable stay in the ground for hundreds or thousands of years, often causing pollution.

broad-leaved type of tree with flat leaves, rather than the thin needle-like leaves of conifers. Most broad-leaved trees, such as maple and oak, lose their leaves in winter.

bromeliad name for any member of a large family of tropical plants. Many are epiphytes, which are plants that grow on other plants.

bud swelling on a plant stem of tiny, young, overlapping leaves or petals and other parts of a flower, ready to burst into bloom

bulb underground bud protected by layers of thick, fleshy leaves. An onion is a type of bulb.

calcium part of food that is vital for healthy growth, especially of the bones and teeth

carbohydrate type of food that gives living things energy

carbon dioxide gas in the air around us that plants use for photosynthesis

cellulose substance found inside the cells of plants. It is a type of carbohydrate and has a structure like fiber.

cholesterol fatty substance. Eating too many foods high in cholesterol can lead to heart disease.

citrus fruit juicy fruit that usually has a thick, spongy rind. Oranges, lemons, grapefruits, and limes are all citrus fruits.

conifer/coniferous kind of tree that has needle-like leaves and seeds that develop in cones

contaminate when something is harmed (made unhealthy) because of contact with something else

cutting part of a plant, such as a leaf, stem, or root, that is used to make more plants

deciduous type of tree or shrub that loses all its leaves in winter

embryo young plant that is contained in a seed

endangered species plant or animal in danger of becoming extinct (dying out)

energy ability in living things to do what they need to do in order to live and grow. Plants and animals get the energy they need from their food.

erosion process by which wind, frost, and rain break rock and soil loose from one area of land and move them to another

ethanol type of alcohol obtained from plant sugars. Ethanol can be used as a fuel.

evaporate/evaporation when water turns from liquid into a vapor (a gas)

evergreen type of plant that does not lose all its leaves at once, but loses some leaves and grows new ones all year round

family group or type of plant

fat nutrient that gives us energy, although too much fat is bad for you. Also, energy storage material in animals.

fertilizer nutrient-rich powder or spray that plant-growers use to increase the amount or quality of their crop

fiber strand of any substance that is long and thin, like thread. We cannot digest fibers in plant parts that we eat, but as they pass through our digestive system they help to keep it healthy.

fruit part of a plant that has seeds inside. Many fruits are good to eat.

germinate when a seed starts to grow roots and shoots in the earliest stage of becoming a plant

habitat place where plants (and animals) live

hardwood another name for broad-leaved trees such as oak and maple. Hardwood trees take much longer to grow than softwood (coniferous) trees.

humid hot and wet

imported when food or goods are brought from one country to be sold in another

infection/infectious when bacteria or other germs spread from one living thing into another and make it sick

iron mineral that is needed for healthy blood

legume family of plants, including peas and beans, that grow their seeds inside pods

mineral substance, such as iron, that is found in some of the foods we eat. Many minerals are good for our health.

nickel type of metal

nutrient type of chemical that nourishes plants and animals

nutritious healthy, full of nutrients

oil greasy substance that does not dissolve in water. Plant oils are very useful.

organism living thing, such as bacteria, cells, plants, and animals

oxygen gas in the air. Plants release oxygen into the air during the process of photosynthesis.

peat partly rotted remains of a plant called bog moss. Peat has proved to be an excellent preservative. Things trapped inside peat can last a very long time without rotting away.

perennial plant that lives for more than two years, often for many years

petal colored part of a flower

photosynthesis process by which a plant produces its food using energy from sunlight, carbon dioxide from the air, and water from the soil

pod capsule that holds the seeds of legume plants, such as peas

pollination when pollen travels from the anthers of one flower to the stigma of the same or a different flower

pollutes/pollution when something poisons or harms any part of the environment (the natural world)

processed when plants are cooked or treated in a certain way to make a new type of food or drink. Apples are processed to make apple juice.

protein substance that is needed for growth, maintenance, and repair

rain forest kind of forest that exists in very hot and wet (rainy) countries of the world

resin sticky sap that flows just beneath a tree's layer of bark

respiration process by which living things release energy from their food

root plant part that anchors plants firmly in the ground and takes in water and nutrients

sap fluid containing food made in the leaves. Sap flows in tubes within a plant's parts, taking food from leaves to the rest of the plant.

seed part of a plant that contains the beginnings of a new plant

shoot new stem growing from the main stem of a plant, or out of a seed

smelt to heat a substance, usually metal ore, in order to obtain usable metal from it

softwood another name for coniferous trees, such as pine and spruce. Softwood trees grow much more quickly than hardwood (broad-leaved) trees.

stalk long, narrow part of a plant that attaches the leaf to the stem. Flower stalks attach little flowers to a stem.

stem part of a plant that holds the plant upright and supports its leaves and flowers

temperate type of climate that is mild, with warmish summers and cool winters. Parts of the United States have a temperate climate.

timber wood that has been cut from a tree to be used in some way

tropics area of the world around the equator with the hottest climate in the world

trunk hard, woody stem of a tree that is covered with bark

tuber short, thick underground stem. New tubers (and, in turn, new plants) can grow from the buds (called "eyes") on a tuber.

turbine machine used to generating power

vapor moisture that is suspended as droplets in air, having changed from a liquid state into a gas, like steam from a kettle

vegetarian someone who chooses not to eat meat or other products made from animals

vitamin type of nutrient in food that helps the body to grow and be protected from illness. The body needs many different types of vitamins.

wind pollinated plants that use wind to carry their pollen from one flower to another

Further Information

Books

Burnie, David. *Eyewitness Guide: Plant*. New York: Dorling Kindersley, 2004.

Burnie, David. *Eyewitness Guide: Tree*. New York: Dorling Kindersley, 2005.

Casper, Julie Kerr. *Natural Resources: Plants*. New York: Chelsea House, 2007.

Hipp, Andrew. *The Green World: Plant Diversity*. New York: Chelsea House, 2007.

Parker, Edward. *Rainforests: Trees and Plants*. Chicago: Raintree, 2003.

Riley, Peter. *Everyday Science: Plants*. Milwaukee: Gareth Stevens, 2004.

Silverstein, Alvin, Virginia Silverstein, and Laura Silverstein Nunn. *Science Concepts Second: Photosynthesis*. Brookfield, Conn.: Twenty-First Century Books, 2007.

Websites

www.mbgnet.net
At Missouri Botanical Garden's website, you can compare the habitats of the world.

www.kew.org/plants/titan/index.html
See the opening of the titan arum bud as well as lots of interesting information about one of the world's smelliest flowers.

www.urbanext.uiuc.edu/gpe/gpe.html
"The Great Plant Escape" is a fun way of learning about what different plant parts do. There is also a simple glossary of terms.

Conservation sites

These sites provide information on the dangers to wild plants and habitats and what conservation groups are doing to help them survive.

www.panda.org
The Worldwide Wildlife Fund works to protect animals and habitats.

www.sierraclub.org
The Sierra Club website provides information about the preservation work carried out by the group.

Places to visit

Many museums, arboretums (botanical gardens devoted to trees), and botanic gardens are fascinating places to visit. You could try:

United States Botanic Garden
245 First Street, S.W.
Washington, DC 20024
www.usbg.gov

New York Botanical Garden
Bronx River Parkway at Fordham Road
Bronx, NY 10458
www.nybg.org

Chicago Botanic Garden
1000 Lake Cook Road
Glencoe, IL 60022
www.chicagobotanic.org

Los Angeles County Arboretum & Botanic Garden
301 North Baldwin Avenue
Arcadia, CA 91007
www.arboretum.org

The State Botanical Garden of Georgia
2450 South Milledge Avenue
Athens, Georgia 30605
www.uga.edu/botgarden

You can also find out about plants by visiting local garden centers. The Latin names of plants will be on the plants' labels, so you can try to find as many related plants as you can.

Index

algae 35
almonds 10
amber 30
aromatherapy 22

bamboo 26, 28, 36, 38
bananas 6, 7, 26
bark 16, 18, 21, 23, 26, 32, 36, 38
barley 12, 43
beans 14–15, 25
belladonna 21
building materials 26–27
bulbs 8, 23

cacao fruit 17
carbohydrates 9, 13
carbon dioxide 4, 5
cellulose 31, 32
cereals 12–13, 43
chillies 17, 18
chocolate drinks 17, 18
cholesterol 11
cinnamon 18, 23
climates 7, 42
clothing 30–31
cloves 18
coal 24–25
coconuts 10, 16, 29
coffee 17
conservation 36–37
contaminated soil 34–35
corn (maize) 12, 25, 43
cotton 31, 33

dried beans 14
drinks 16–17, 40

energy 4, 5, 7, 9, 10, 13, 24, 25
erosion 37
ethanol 25
eucalyptus 20, 23

fabrics 30, 31
fats 10, 17, 34
fibers 7, 29, 30, 31, 32, 33, 38
flavorings 18–19
flooring 29
food chains 4, 40

fossil fuels 24–25
foxgloves 20
fruits 6–7, 8, 10, 16, 23, 41, 42
fuel 24–25

garlic 23
gas 24, 25
ginger 18
ginseng 21
grains 12, 13
grapes 6, 7
grasses 12, 26, 37, 43

hardwoods 27, 28, 38, 42
herbs 18–19
houseplants 29

kidney beans 14

lavender 22
legumes 14, 15
leisure activities 38–39
lungwort 20

medicinal plants 20–21, 23
milk-tree 16
millet 12, 43
minerals 9

nickel mining 35
nutrients 9, 35, 37
nuts 10–11

oats 12, 43
oil (petroleum) 24, 25
oils 7, 11, 20, 22–23, 25, 34
oranges 6, 7, 22, 23, 41
oxygen 5, 35

palms 30, 34
pandas 36
paper 32–33
peanuts 10
peas 14, 15
peat 24, 25
peppercorns 18
perennial plants 19
perfumes 22, 23, 40–41
photosynthesis 4, 5, 9, 24, 35

pods 10, 14, 15, 17, 31
pollination 13, 22
pollution 5
poppies 21
potatoes 8, 9
proteins 10, 13, 14, 43

rain forests 28, 38
reeds 26, 32, 35
resin 30, 33
respiration 5
rice 12, 13, 43
roots 8, 21, 35, 37
rubber 38
rye 12, 13, 43

sap 16, 21, 27, 38
sea vegetables 9
seeds 6, 7, 8, 10, 11, 12, 13, 14, 17, 18, 31, 43
sesame seeds 11, 34
sewage systems 35
soap 34
softwoods 27, 32, 42
sorghum 43
soybeans 15, 25, 34
spices 18
stalks 8, 18, 26
stems 6, 9, 15, 18, 21, 22, 26, 28, 30, 35, 36
straw 26, 33
sugar beet 19
sugar cane 19, 25
sugars 4, 7, 25
sunflower seeds 11

tea 16
tea trees 23
timber 27, 28, 32
trees 5, 26, 27, 28, 30, 32, 33, 36, 37, 38, 42

vegetables 8–9, 25, 41, 42
vitamins 7, 9, 14, 18, 43

wheat 12, 13, 43
wood 24, 26–27, 28, 32, 38

yew 20